Shri Ram Charit Manas-S

|| Shalok ||

Shaantan shaashvatamaprameyamanaghan
nirvaanashaantipradan.
Brahmaashambhuphaneendrasevyamanishan vedaantavedyan
vibhum.
Raamaakhyan jagadeeshvaran suragurun maayaamanushyan
harin.
Vandehan karunaakaran raghuvaran bhoopaalachoodaamanim
||1||

Naanya sprha raghupate hrdayesmadeeye.
Satyan vadaami ch bhavaanakhilaantaraatma.
Bhaktin prayachchh raghupungav nirbharaan me.
Kaamaadidosharahitan kuru maanasan ch ||2||

Atulitabaladhaaman hemashailaabhadehan.
Danujavanakrshaanun gyaaninaamagraganyam.
Sakalagunanidhaanan vaanaraanaamadheeshan.

|| Chopai ||

Jaamavant ke bachan suhae. suni hanumant hrday ati bhae.
Tab lagi mohi parikhehu tumh bhaee. sahi dukh kand mool phal
khaee.
Jab lagi aavaun seetahi dekhee. hoihi kaaju mohi harash
biseshee.
Yah kahi nai sabanhi kahun maatha. chaleu harashi hiyan dhari
raghunaatha.

Sindhu teer ek bhoodhar sundar. kautuk koodi chadheu ta oopar.

Baar-baar raghubeer sanbhaaree. tarakeu pavanatanay bal bhaaree.

Jehin giri charan dei hanumanta. chaleu so ga paataal turanta.

Jimi amogh raghupati kar baana. ehee bhaanti chaleu hanumaana.

Jalanidhi raghupati doot bichaaree. tain mainaak hohi shram haaree.

|| Doha – 1 ||

Hanumaan tehi parasa kar puni keenh pranaam |
Raam kaaju keenhe binu mohi kahaa bishraam ||

||Chopai||

Jaat pavansut devanh dekha | Jaanai kahu bal buddhi bisesha ||
Surasa naam ahinh kai maata | Pathainhi aai kahi tehi baata ||
Aaju suranh mohi deenh ahaara | Sunat bachan kah pavankumaara ||
Raam kaaju kari phiri mai aavau | Sita kai sudhi prabhuhi sunaavau ||
Tab tav badan paithihau aai | Satya kahau mohi jaan de maai ||
Kavanehu jatan dei nahi jaana | Grasai na mohi kaheu Hanumaana||
Jojan bhari tehi badanu pasaara | Kapi tanu keenh dugun Bistaaraa||
Sorah jojan mukh tehi thayau | Turat pavan sut battis bhayau ||
Jas jas surasa badanu badhaava | Taasu doon kapi roop dekhaava ||
Sat jojan tehi aanan keenha | Ati laghu roop pavanasut leenha

||
Badan paithi puni baaher aava | Maaga bida taahi siru naava ||
Mohi suranh jehi laagi pathaava | Buddhi bal maramu tor mai
paava||

|| Doha – 2 ||

Raam kaaju sabu karihahu tumh bal buddhi nidhaan|
Aasish dei gai so harashi chaleu Hanumaan ||

||Chopai||

Nisichari ek sindhu mahu rahai |Kari maaya nabhu ke khag
gahai||
Jeev jantu je gagan udaahi |Jal biloki tinh kai parichhahi ||
Gahai chhah sak so na udaai |Ehi bidhi sada gaganchar khaai ||
Soi chhal Hanumaan kah keenha|Taasu kapatu kapi turatahi
cheena||
Taahi maari maarut sut beera|Baaridhi paar gayau
matidheera||
Taha jaai dekhi ban sobha|Gunjat chanchareek madhu lobha||
Naana taru phal phool suhaae|Khag mrug brund dekhi man
bhaae||
Sail bisaal dekhi ek aage | Taa par dhaai chadheu bhay tyaage
||
Uma na kachhu kapi kai adhikaai | Prabhu prataap jo kaalahi
khaai ||
Giri par chadhi Lanka tehi dekhi| Kahi na jaai ati durg biseshi ||
Ati utang jalanidhi chahu paasa|
Kanak kot kar param prakaasa||

|| Chhand ||

Kanak kot bichitra mani | Krut sundaraayatana Ghana||
Chauhatt hatt subatt beethee Chaaru pur bahu bidhi bana||
Gaj baaji khachchar nikar Padchar rath baroothanhi ko ganai|
Bahuroop nisichar jooth atibal Sen baranat nahin banai ||1||
Ban bag ujpaban baatika| Sar koop baapee sohahi||
Nar naag sur gandharb kanya| Roop muni man mohahee||
Kahu maal deh bisaal sai l Samaan atibal garjahi||
Naana akhaarenh bhirhi bahubidhi Ek ekanh tarjahee ||2||
Kari jatan bhat kotinh bikat Tan nagar chahu disi rachchhahee||
Kahu mahish maanush dhenu khar Ajakhal nishaachar
bhachchhahi||
Ehi laagi Tulasidaas inh kee Katha kachhu ek hai kahee |
Raghubeer sar teerath sareeranhi Tyaagi gati paihahi sahee||

|| Doha – 3 ||

Pur rakhavaare dekhi bahu kapi man keenh bichaar|
Ati laghu roop dharau nisi nagar karau paisaar ||

||Chopai||

Masak samaan roop kapi charee | Lankahi chaleu sumiri
naraharee||
Naam Lankinee ek nisicharee | So kah chalesi mohi nindaree ||
Jaanehi nahee maramu sath mora| Mor ahar jahaa lagi chora ||
Muthika ek maha kapi hanee | Rudhir bamat dharanee
dhanamanee ||
Puni sambhari uthee so Lanka | Jori paani kar binay sasanka ||
Jab Ravanahi brahm bar deenha | Chalat biranchi kaha mohi
cheenha ||
Bikal hosi tai kapi ke mare | Tab jaanesu nisichar sanghare ||
Taat mor ati punya bahoota | Dekheu nayan Raam kar doota |

|| Doha – 4 ||

Taat swarg apabarg sukh dharia tula ek ang |
Tool na taahi sakal mili jo such lav satsang ||

||Chopai||

Prabisi nagar keeje sab kaaja | Hriday rakhi kosalapur raja ||
Garal sudha ripu karahi mitaai | Gopad sindhu anal sitalaai ||
Garud sumeru renu sam taahi | Raam krupa kari chitava jaahi ||

Ati laghu roop dhareu Hamumaana | Paitha ngar sumiri bhagawana ||
Mandir mandir prati kari sodha | Dekhe jah tah aganit jodha ||
Gayau dasaanan mandir maahee | Ati bichitra kahi jaat so naahee ||
Sayan kie dekha kapi tehee | Mandir mahu na deekhi baidehee ||
Bhavan ek puni deekh suhaava | Hari mandir tah bhinna banaava ||

|| Doha – 5 ||

Raamaayudh ankit gruh sobha barani na jaai |
Nav tulsika brund tah dekhi harash kapiraai||

||Chopai||

Lanka nisichar nikar nivaasa | Iha kaha sajjan kar baasa ||
Man mahu tarak karai kapi laaga | Tehi samay |Bibheeshanu jaaga ||
Raam raam tehi sumiran keenha | Hriday harash kapi sajjan cheenha ||

Ehi san hathi karihau pahichaanee |
Saadhu te hoi na kaaraj haanee ||

Bipra roop dhari bachan sunaae | Sunat Bibheeshan uthi tah aae ||
Kari pranaam poonchee kusalaai | Bipra kahahu nij katha buzaai ||
Kee tumh hari daasanh mah koi | More hriday preeti ati hoi ||
Kee tumh raamu deen anuraagee | Aayahu mohi karan badbhaagee ||

|| Doha – 6 ||

Tab Hanumant kahee sab Raam katha nij naam |
Sunat jugal tan pulak man magan sumiri gun graam||

||Chopai||

Sunahu pavansut rahani hamaaree | Jimi dasananhi mahu jeebh bichaaree ||
Taat kabahu mohi jaani anaatha | Karihahi krupa bhaanukul naatha ||
Taamas tanu kachu saadhan naahee |
Preeti na pad saroj man maahee ||
Ab mohi bha bharos Hanumanta |

Binu harikrupa milahi nahi santa ||
Jau Rabhubeer anugrah keenha | Tau tumh mohi darasu hathi deenha ||
Sunahu Bibheeshan prabhu kai reetee | Karahi sada sevak par preetee ||
Kahahu kavan mai param kuleena | Kapi chanchal sabahee bidhi heena ||
Praat lei jo naam hamaara | Tehi din taahi na milai ahaara ||

|| Doha – 7 ||

As mai adham sakha sunu mohu par Rabhubeer |
Keenhee krupa sumiri gun bhare bilochan neer ||

||Chopai||

Jaanatahoo as swami bisaaree |
Phirhi te kaahe na hohi dukharee ||
Ehi bidhi kahat Raam gun graama |
Paava anirbachya bishraama ||
Puni sab katha Bibheeshan kahi |
Jehi bidhi Janakasuta tah rahee ||
Tab Hanumant kaha sunu bhraata |

Dekhi chahau Jaanaki Maata ||
Juguti Bibheeshan sakal sunaai | Chaleu pavansut bida karaai ||
Kari soi roop gayau puni tahava |
Ban Asok Sita rah jahava ||
Dekhi manahi mahu keenh pranaama | Baithehi beeti jaat nisi
jaama ||
Krus tanu sees jata ek benee |
Japati hraday Raghupati gun shrenee ||

|| Doha – 8 ||

Nij pad nayan die man Raam pad kamal leen |
Param dukhee bha pavansut dekhi Jaanakee deen ||

||Chopai||

Taru pallav mahu rahaa lukaai |
Karai bichaar karau kaa bhai ||
Tehi avasar Raavanu tah aava | Sang naari bahu kie banaava ||

Bahu bidhi khal Sitahi samuzaava | Saam daam bhay bhed dekhaava ||
Kah Ravanu sunu sumukhi sayaanee | Mandodari aadi sab raanee ||

Tav anucharee karau pan mora | Ek baar bilku mam ora ||
Trun dhari ot kahati baidehee | Sumiri avadhapati param sanehe ||
Sunu dasamukh khadyot prakasa | Kabahu ki nalinee karai bikaasa ||
As man samuzu kahati Jaanakee | Khal sudhi nahi Rabhubeer baan kee ||
Sath soone hari aanehi mohee | Adham nilajj laaj nahi tohee ||
|| Doha – 9 ||
Aapuhi suni khadyot sam Ramahi bhaanu samaan |
Parush bachan suni kaadhi asi bola ati khisiaan ||

||Chopai||
Sita tai mam krut apamaanaa |
Katihau tav sir kathin krupaanaa ||
Naahi ta sapadi maanu mam baanee |
Sumukhi hoti na ta jeevan haanee ||
Syaam saroj daam sam sundar |
Prabhu bhuj kari kar sam dasakandhar ||
So bhuj kanth ki tav asi ghora |

Sunu sath as pravaan pan mora ||
Chandrahaas haru mam paritaapam |
Rathupati birah anal sanjaatam ||
Sital nisit bahasi bar dhaara |
Kah Sita haru mam dukh bhaara ||

Sunat bachan puni maaran dhaava | Mayatanaya kahi neeti buzaava ||
Kahsi sakal nisicharanhi bolaai | Sitahi bahu bidhi traasahu jaai ||
Maas divas mahu kahaa na maana | Tau mai maarabi kaadhi krupaana ||

|| Doha – 10 ||

Bhavan gayau daskandhar iha pisaachini brund |
Sitahi traas dekhaavahi dharahi roop bahu mand||

||Chopai||

Trijata naam rachchhasi eka| Raam charan rati nipun bibeka||
Sabanhau boli sunaaesi sapana | Sitahi sei karahu hit apana ||
Sapane baanar Lanka jaari | Jaatudhaan sena sab maaree||
Khar aarudh nagan dasaseesa| Mundit sir khandit bhuj beesa||

Ehi bidhi so dachchhin disi jaai| Lanka manahu Bibheeshan paai||
Nagar phiri Rabhubeer dohaai| Tab prabhu Sita boli pathaai||
Yah sapana mai kahau pukaaree| Hoihi satya gae din chaaree||
Taasu bachan suni te sab daree| Janaksuta ke charananhi paree||

|| Doha – 11 ||

Jah tah gai sakal tab Sita kar man soch|
Maas divas beete mohi maarihi nisichar poch||

||Chopai||

Trijata san bolee kar joree | Maatu bipati sangini tai more ||
Tajau deh karu begi upaai| Dusah birahu ab nahi sahi jaai||
Aani kaath rachu chita banaai | Maatu anal puni dehi lagaai||

Satya karahi mam preeti sayaanee | Sunai ko Shravan sool sam baanee ||
Sunat bachan pad gahi samuzaaesi| Prabhu prataap bal sujasu sunaaesi||
Nisi na anal mil sunu sukumaaree| As kah so nij bhavan sidhaaree||
Kah Sita bidhi bha pratikula| Milihi na paavak mitihi na soola||
Dekhiat pragat gagan angaara| Avani na aavat ekau taara||

Paavakmay sasi sravat na aagee| Maanahu mohi jaani hatabhaagee||
Sunahi binay mam bitap asoka| Satya naam karu haru mam soka||
Nootan kisalay anal samaana| Dehi agini jani karahi nidaana||
Dekhi param birahaakul sita| So chhan kapihi kalap sam beeta||
|| Doha – 12 ||
Kapi kari hriday bichaar deenhi mudrika daari tab|
Janu asok angaar deenh harashi uthi kar gaheu||

||Chopai||
Tab dekhee mudrika manohar | Raam naam ankit ati sundar ||
Chakit chitav mudaree pahichanee |
Harash bishaad hriday akulaanee||
Jeeti ko sakai ajay Raghuraai|
Maaya te asi rachi nahi jaai||
Sita man bichaar kar nana|
Madhur bachan boleu Hanumaana||
Raamchandra gun baranai laaga| Sunatahi Sita kar bukh bhaaga||

Laagee sunai shravan man laai| Aadihu te sab katha sunaai||
Shravanaamrut jehi katha suhaai| Kahi so pragat hoti kin bhaai||
Tab Hunamant nikat chali gayau| Phiri baithee man bisamay bhayau||
Raam doot mai maatu Jaanakee| Satya sapath karunaanidhaan kee ||
Yah mudrika maatu mai aanee| Deenhi Raam tumh kah sahidaanee||
Nar baanarahi sang kahu kaise|
Kahi katha bhai sangati jaise||
|| Doha – 13 ||
Kapi ke bachan saprem suni upaja man biswaas|
Jaana man kram bachan yah krupaasindhu kar daas||

||Chopai||
Harijan jaani preeti ati gaadhee|
Sajal nayan pulakaavali baadhee||
Budat birah jaladhi Hanumaana|
Bhayahu taat mo kahu jalajaana||
Ab kahu kusal jaau balihaaree|

Anuj sahit such bhavan kharaaree||
Komalchit krupaal Raghuraai| Kapi kehi hetu dharee nithuraai||
Sahaj baani sevak sukhdaayak|
Kabahuk surati karat Raghunaayak||
Kabahu nayan mam Sital taata|
Hoihahi nirakhi syaam mrudu gaata||
Bachanu na aav nayan bhare baaree| Ahah naath hau nipat bisaree||

Dekhi param birahaakul Sita| Bola kapi mrudu bachan bineeta||
Maatu kusal prabhu anuj sameta| Tav dukh dukhi sukrupa niketa||
Jani jananee maanahu jiy oona| Tumh te premu raam ke doona||

|| Doha – 14 ||

Raghupati kar sandesu ab sunu jananee dhari dheer|
As kahi kapi gadagad bhayau bhare bilochan neer||

||Chopai||

Kaheu Raam biyog tav Sita| Mo kahu sakal bhae bipareeta||
Nav taru kisalay manahu krusaanu| Kaalanisa sam nisi sasi bhaanoo||

Kubalay bipin kunt ban sarisa| Baarid tapat tel janu barisa||
Je hit rahe karat tei peera| Urag swaas sam tribidh sameera||
Kahehoo te kachoo dukh ghati hoi| Kaahi kahau yah jaan na koi||
Tatva prem kar mam aru tora| Jaant priya eku manu mora||
So manu sada rahat tohi paahee| Jaanu preeti rasu etanehi maahee||
Prabhu sandesu sunat baidehee| Magan prem tan sudhi nahi tehee||
Kah kapi hriday dheer dharu maata| Sumiru Raam sevak sukhdaata||
Ur aanahu Raghupati prabhutaai| Sun imam bachan tajahu kadaraai||

||Doha – 15 ||

Nisichar nikar patang sam Raghupati baan krusanu|
Jananee hriday dheer dharu jare nisaachar jaanu||

||Chopai||

Jau Raghubeer hoti sudhi paai|
Karate nahi bilambu Raghuraai||
Raam baan rabi ue Jaanakee|

Tam barooth kah jaatudhaan kee||
Abahi maatu mai jaau lavaai|
Prabhu aayasu nahi Raam dohaai||
Kachhuk divas jananee dharu dheera|
Kapinh sahit aihahi Rabhubeera||
Nisichar maari tohi lai jaihahi|
Tihu pur Naaradaadi jasu gaihahi||
Hai sut kapi sab tumhahi samaana|
Jatudhaan ati bhat balawaana||
More hriday param sandeha|
Suni kapi pragat keenhi nij deha||
Kanak bhudharaakaar sareera|
Samar bhayankar atibal beera||
Sita man bharos tab bhayaoo| Puni laghu roop pavanasut layaoo||

|| Doha – 16 ||

Sunu maata saakhaamrug nahi bal buddhi bisaal|
Prabhu prataap te garudahi khaai param laghu byaal||

||Chopai||

Man santosh sunat kapi baanee| Bhagati prataap tej bal saanee||
Aashish deenhi raampriy jaana| Hohu taat bal seel nidhaana||
Ajar amar gunanidhi sut hohu| Karahu bahut Raghunaayak chhohoo||

Karahu krupa prabhu as suni kaana| Nirbhar prem magan Hanumaana||

Baar baar naaesi pad seesa| Bola bachan jori kar keesa||

Ab krutkrutya bhayau mai maata| Aasish tav amogh bikhyaata||

Sunahu maatu mohi atisay bhookha| Laagi dekhi sundar phal rookha||

Sunu sut karahi bipin rakhawaaree| Param subhat rajaneechar bhaaree||

Tinh kar bhay maata mohi naahee| Jau tumh such maanahu man maahee||

|| Doha – 17 ||

Dekhi buddhi bal nipun kapi kaheu Jaankee jaahu|

Raghupati charan hriday dhari taat madhur phal khaahu||

||Chopai||

Chaleu naai siru paitheu baaga| Phal khaaesi taru torai laaga||

Rahe taha bahu bhat rakhawaare| Kachhu maaresi kachhu jaai pukaare||

Naath ek aava kapi bhaaree | Tehi Asok baatika ujaaree||

Khaaesi phal aru bitap upaare| Rachchhak mardi mardi mahi dare||

Suni Raavan pathae bhat nana| Tinhahi dekhi garjeu Hanumaana||

Sab rajanichar kapi sanghaare| Gae pukaarat kachhu adhamaare||

Puni pathayau tehi achchhakumaara| Chala sang lai subhat apaara||

Aavat dekhi bitap gahi tarja|

Taahi nipaati mahaadhuni garja||

|| Doha – 18 ||

Kachhu maaresi kachhu mardesi kachhu milaesi dhari dhoori|
Kachu puni jaai pukaare prabhu markat bal bhori||

||Chopai||

Chala Indrajit atulit jodha|
Bandhu nidhan suni upaja krodha||
Kapi dekha daarun bhat aava|
Katakataai garja aru dhaava||
Ati bisaal taru ek upaara|
Birath keenh Lankes kumara||
Rahe mahaabhat taake sanga|
Gahi gahi kapi mardai nij anga||
Tinhahi nipaati taahi san baaja|
Bhire jugal maanahu gajaraaja||
Muthika maari chadha taru jaai| Taahi ek chhan muruchha aai||
Uthi bahori keenhisi bahu maaya| Jeeti na jaai prabhanjan jaaya||

|| Doha – 19 ||

Brahm astra tehi saandha kapi man keenh bichaar|
Jau na brahmasar maanau mahima mitai apaar||

||Chopai||

Brahmabaan kapi kahu tehi maara|
Paratihu baar kataku sanghaara||

Tehi dekha kapi muruchhit bhayau| Naagpaas baandhesi lai gayau||

Jaasu naam japi sunahu bhavaanee|
Bhav bandhan kaatahi nar gyaanee||
Taasu doot ki bandh taru aava| Prabhu kaaraj lagi kapihi bandhava||
Kapibandhan suni nisichar dhaae| Kautuk laagi sabha sab aae||
Dasamukh sabha deekhi kapi jaai| Kahi na jaai kachhu ati prabhutaai||
Kar jore sur disip bineeta| Bhrukuti bilokat sakal sabheeta||
Dekhi prataap na kapi man sanka|
Jimi ahigan mahu garud asanka||

|| Doha – 20 ||

Kapihi biloki dasaanan bihasa kahi durbaad|
Sutabadh surati keenhi puni upaja hriday bishaad||

||Chopai||

Kah Lankes kavan tai keesa|
Kehi ke bal ghalehi ban kheesa||
Kee dhau Shravan sunehi nahi mohee|

Dekhau ati asank sath tohee||
Maare nisichar kehi aparaadha|
Kahu sath tohi na praan kai baadha||
Sunu Raavan brahmaand nikaaya|
Paai jaasu bal birachati maaya||
Jaake bal biranchi hari isa| Paalat srujat harat dasaseesa||
Jaa bal sees dharat sahasaanan| Andakos samet giri kaanan||
Dharat jo bibidh deh suratraata| Tumh se sathanh sikhaavanu data||

Har kodand kathin jehi bhanja| Tehi samet nrup dal mad ganja||

Khar dushan trisira aru baalee| Badhe sakal atulit balasaalee||

|| Doha – 21 ||

Jaake bal lavales te jitehu charaachar zaari|

Taasu doot mai jaa kari hari aanehu priy naari||

||Chopai||

Jaanau mai tumhaari prabhutaai| Sahasabaahu san paree laraai||

Samar baali san kari jasu paava| Suni kapi bachan bihasi biharaava||

Khayau phal prabhu laagi bhookha|

Kapi subhaav te toreu rookha||

Sab ke deh param priy swaamee|

Maarahi mohi kumaarag gaamee||

Jinh mohi maara te mai mare|

Tehi par bandheu tanay tumhaare||

Binati karau jori kar raavan|

Sunahu maan taji mor sikhaavan||

Dekhahu tumh nij kulahi bichaaree|

Bhram taji bhajahu bhagat bhay haaree||

Jaake dar ati kaal deraai|

Jo sur asur charaachar khaai||

Taaso bayaru kabahu nahi keejai | More kahe Jaanakee deejay||

|| Doha – 22 ||

Pranatapaal Raghunaayak karuna Sindhu kharaari|

Gae saran prabhu raakhihai tav aparaadh bisaari||

||Chopai||

Raam charan Pankaj ur dharahoo|
Lanka achal raaju tumh karahoo||
Rishi pulasti jasu bimal mayanka|
Tehi sasi mahu jani hohu kalanka||
Raam naam binu gira na soha|
Dekhu bichari tyagi mad moha||
Basan heen nahi soh suraree|
Sab bhushan bhushit bar naaree||
Raam bimukh sampati prabhutaai | Jaai rahi paai binu paai ||
Sajal mool jinh saritanh nahi | Barashi gae puni tabahi sukhahee ||
Sunu dasakanth kahau pan ropee | Bimukh Raam traata nahi kopee ||
Sankar sahas bishnu aj tohee | Sakahi na raakhi raam kar drohee ||

|| Doha – 23 ||

Mohmool bahu sool prad tyagahu tam abhimaan|
Bhajahu Raam Raghunaayak krupa sindhu Bhagawaan ||

||Chopai||

Jadapi kahee kapi ati hit baanee| Bhagati bibek birati nay saanee ||
Bola bihasi maha abhimaanee| Mila hahahi kapi gur bad gyanee||
Mrutyu nikat aai khal tohee| Laagesi adham sikhaavan mohee||
Ulata hoihi kah Hanumaana| Matibhram tor pragat mai jaana|
Suni kapi bachan bahut khisiaana| Begi na harahu moodh ka praana||

Sunat nisaachar maaran dhaae| Sachivanh sahit Bibheeshanu aae||

Naai sees kari binay bahoota| Neeti birodh na maaria doota||

Aan dand kachhu karia gosaai| Sabahee kahaa mantra bhal bhai||

Sunat bihasi bola daskandhar | Ang bhang kari pathaia Bandar ||

|| Doha – 24 ||

kapi ke mamata poonch par sabahi kahau samuzaai|

Tel bori pat baandhi puni paavak dehu lagaai ||

||Chopai||

Poonchh-heen baanar tah jaaehi| Tab sath nij naathhi lai aaihi ||

Jinh kai keenhisi bahut badaai| Dekhu mai tinh kai prabhutaai ||

Bachan sunat kapi man musukaana|

Bhai sahaay saarad mai jaana ||

Jaatudhaan suni Raavan bachana|

Laage rachai moodh soi rachana||

Raha na nagar basan ghrut tela|

Baadhee poonch keenh kapi khela||

Kautik kah aae purbaasee|

Maarahi charan karahi bahu haasee||

Baajahi dhol dehi sab taaree |

Nagar pheri puni poonch prajaaree||

Paavak jaat dekhi Hanumanta| Bhayau param lafghuroop turanta||

Nibuki chadheu kapi kanak ataaree | Bhai sabheet nisaachar naaree ||

|| Doha – 25 ||

Hari prerit tehi avasar chale marut unachaas|
Attahaas kari garja kapi badhi laag akaas||

||Chopai||

Deh bisaal param haruaai|
Mandir te mandir chadh dhaai||
Jarai nagar bha log bihaala|
Zapat lapat bahu koti karaala||
Taat maatu haa sunia pukaara|
Ehi avasar ko hamahi ubaara||
Ham jo kaha yah kapi nahi hoi|
Baanar roop dhare sur koi ||
Saadhu avagya kar phalu aisa|
Jarai nagar anaath kar jaisa||
Jaara nagaru nimish ek maahee|
Ek Bibheeshan kar bruh naahee ||
Taa kar doot anal jehi sirija |
Jaraa na so tehi kaaran girija ||
Ulati palati Lanka sab Jaaree |
Koodi para puni sindhu mazaaree ||

|| Doha – 26 ||

Poonch buzaai khoi shram dhari laghu roop bahori|
Janaksuta ke aage thaadh bhayau kar jori ||

||Chopai||

Maatu mohi deeje kachhu cheenha |
Jaise Raghunaayak mohi deenha ||

Choodamani utaari tab dayaoo |
Harash samet pavanasut layaoo | |
Kahehu taat as mor pranaama|
Sab prakaar prabhu pooranakaama| |
Deen dayaal biridu sambhaaree|
Harahu naath mam sankat bhaaree| |
Taat sakrasut katha sunaaehu| Baan prataap prabhuhi
samuzaehu| |
Maas divas mahu naath na aava|
Tau puni mohi jiat nahi paava| |
Kahu kapi kehi bidhi rakhau praana|
Tumhahoo Taat kahat ab jaana| |
Tohi dekhi seetali bhai chhatee| Puni mo kahu soi dinu so
raatee| |

|| Doha – 27 ||

Janakasutahi samuzaai kari bahu bidhi dheeraju deenh|
Charan kamal siru naai kapi gavanu Raam pahi keenh | |

||Chopai||

Chalat mahaadhuni garjesi bhaaree |
Garbh stravahi suni nisichar naaree | |
Naaghi sindhu ehi paarahi aava |
Sabad kilikila kapinh sunaava | |
Harashe sab biloki Hanumaana | Nutan janm kapinh tab jaana
| |
Mukh prasanna tan tej biraaja |
Keenhesi raamachandra kar kaaja | |
Mile sakal ati bhae sukhaaree |
Talafat meen paav jimi baaree | |
Chale harashi Raghunaayak paasa | Poonchhat kahat naval

itihaasa ||
Tab madhuban bheetar sab aae| Angad sammat madhu phal khaae||
Rakhawaare jab barajan laage| Mushti prahaar hanta sab bhaage

|| Doha – 28 ||
Jaai pukaare te sab ban ujaar jubaraaj |
Suni Sugreev harash kapi kari aae prabhu kaaj ||

||Chopai||
Jau na hoti sita sudhi paai | Madhuban ke fal sakahi ki khaai ||
Ehi bidhi man bichaar kar raja | Aai gae kapi sahit samaaja ||
Aai sabanhi naava pad seesa | Mileu sabanhi ati prem kapeesa||
Poonchhee kusal kusal pad dekhee| Raam krupa bhaa kaaju biseshee ||
Naath kaaju keenheu Hanumaana | Raakhe sakal kapinh ke praana ||
Suni Sugreev bahuri tehi mileu | Kapinh sahit Raghupati pahi chaleoo||
Raam kapinh jab aavat dekha | Kie kaaju man harash bisesha |
Fatik sila baithe dwau bhaai | Pare sakal kapi charanhi jaai ||

|| Doha – 29 ||
Preeti sahit sab bhete Raghupati karuna punj|
Poonchhee kusal naath ab kusal dekhi pad kanj||

||Chopai||
Jaamvant kah sunu Raghuraaya |
Jaa par naath karahu tumh daaya ||

Taahi sada subh kusal nirantar |
Sur nar muni prasannata upar ||
Soi bijai binai gun saagar |
Taasu sujasu trailok ujaagar ||
Prabhu kee krupa bhayau sabu kaaju |
Janma hamaar safal bhaa aaju ||
Naath pavansut keenhi jo karanee | Sahasahu much na jaai so
baranee ||
Pavantanay ke charit suhaae |
Jaamavant Raghupatihi sunaae ||
Sunat krupaanidhi man ati bhaae | Puni Hanumaan harashi hiy
laae ||
Kahahu taat kehi bhaanti Jaanakee |
Rahati karati rachchha swapraan kee ||

|| Doha – 30 ||

Naam paaharu divas nisi dhyaan tumhaar kapaat |
Lochan nij pad jantrit jaahi praan kehi baat ||

||Chopai||

Chalat mohi choodaamani deenhee |
Raghupati hriday laai soi leenhee ||
Naath jugal lochan bhari baree |
Bachan kahe kachhu Janakkumari ||
Anuj samet gahehu prabhu charana |
Deen bandhu pranataarati harana ||
Man kram bachan charan anuraagee |
Kehi aparaadh naath hau tyaagee ||
Avagun ek mor mai maana |
Bichhurat praan na keenh payaana ||

Naath so nayananhi ko aparaadha | Nisarat praan karahi hathi baadha ||
Birah agini tanu tool sameera |
Swaas jarai chhan maahi sareera ||
Nayan stravahi jalu nij hit laagee |

Jarai na paav deh birahaagee ||
Sita kai ati bipati bisaala | Binahi kahe bhali deendayaala ||

|| Doha – 31 ||

Ninish nimish karunaanidhi jaahi kalap sam beeti|
Begi chalia prabhu aania bhuj bal khal dal jeeti ||

||Chopai||

Suni Sita dookh prabhu sukh ayana| Bhari aae jal raajiv nayana ||
Bachan kaay man mam gati jaahee | Sapanehu boozia bipati ki taahee ||
Kah Hanumant bipati prabhu soi| Jab tav sumiran bhajan na ho ||
Ketik baat prabu jaatudhaan kee | Ripuhi jeeti aanibee jaankee ||
Sunu kapi tohi samaan upakaaree | Nahi kou sur nar muni tanudhaaree ||
Prati upakaar karau kaa tora| Sanmukh hoi na sakat man mora ||
Sunu sut tohi urin mai naahee | Dekheu kari bichaar man maahee ||
Puni puni kapihi chitav surtraata | Lochan neer pulak ati gaata ||

|| Doha – 32 ||

Suni prabhu bachan biloki mukh gaat harashi Hanumant|
Charan pareu premaakul traahi traahi bhagavant ||

||Chopai||

Baar baar prabhu chahai uthaava |
Prem magan tehi uthab na bhaava ||
Prabhu kar pankaj kapi ke seesa |
Sumiri so dasa magan gaureesa ||
Saavadhaan man kari puni sankar |
Laage kahan katha ati sundar ||
Kapi uthaai prabhu hriday lagaava |
Kar gahi param nikat baithaava ||
Kahu kapi Raavan paalit Lanka |
Kehi bidhi daheu durg a ti banka ||
Prabhu prasanna jaana Hanumaana |
Bola bachan bigat abhimaana ||
Saakhaamrug kai badi manusaai | Saakha te saakha par jaai ||
Naaghi sindhu haatkapur jaara | Nisichar gan badhi bipin ujaara ||

So sab tav prataap Raghuraai |
Naath na kachoo mori prabhutaai ||

|| Doha – 33 ||

Taa kahu prabhu kachhu agam nahi jaa par tumh anukool|
Tav prabhaav badavaanalahi jaari sakai khalu tool||

||Chopai||

Naath bhagati ati sukhadaayanee | Dehu krupa kari anapaayanee ||
Suni prabhu param saral kapi baanee |
Evamastu tab kaheu bhavaanee ||
Uma Raam subhaau jehi jaana |
Taahi bhajanu taji bhaav na aana ||
Yah sambaad jaasu ur aava |
Raghupati charan bhagati soi paava ||
Suni prabhu bachan kahahi kapibrunda |
Jay Jay Jay krupaal sukhkanda ||
Tab Raghupati kapipatihi bolaava |

Kaha chalai kar karahu banaava ||
Ab bilambu kehi kaaran keeje |
Turat kapinh kahu aayasu deeje ||
Kautuk dekhi suman bahu barashi |
Nabh te bhavan chale sur harashee ||

|| Doha – 34 ||

Kapipati begi bolaae aae juthap jooth |
Naana baran atul bal baanar bhaalu barooth ||

||Chopai||

Prabhu pad pankaj naavahi seesa |
Garjahi bhaalu mahaabal keesa ||
Dekhi Raam sakal kapi sena |
Chitai krupa kari Raajiv naina ||
Raam krupa bal paai kapinda |
Bhae pachchhajut manahu girinda ||
Harashi Raam tab keenh payaana |

Sagun bhae sundar subh nana ||
Jaasu sakal mangalamay keetee |
Taasu payaan sagun yah neetee ||
Prabhu payaan jaana baidehee |
Faraki baam ang janu kahi dehee ||
Joi joi sagun jaanakihi hoi |
Asagun bhayau Raavanahi soi ||
Chala kataku ko baranai paara |
Garjahi baanar bhaalu apaara ||
Nakh aayudh giri paadapadhaaree |
Chale gagan mahi ichchhachaaree ||
Ke harinaad bhaalu kapi karahee |
Dagamagaahi diggaj chikkarahee ||

|| Chhand ||

Chikkarahi diggaj dol Mahi giri lol saagar kharabhare |
Man harash sabh gandharb sur Muni naag kinnar dukh tare ||

Katakatahi markat bikat bhat Bahu koti kotinh dhaavahee |
Jay Raam prabal prataap Kosalnaath gun gan gaavahee ||1||
Sahi sak na bhaar udaar Ahipati baar baarhi mohai ||
Gah dasan puni puni Kamath Prushth kathor so kimi sohai ||
Rabhubeer ruchir prayaan prasthiti Jaani param suhaavanee |
Janu kamath kharpar sarparaaj so Likhat abichal paavanee
||2||

|| Doha – 35 ||

Ehi bidhi jaai krupaanidhi utare saagar teer|
Jah tah laage khaan fal bhaalu bipul kapi beer||

||Chopai||

Uhaa nisaachar rahahi sasanka|
Jab te jaari gayau kapi Lanka ||
Nij nij gruh sab karahi bichaara |
Nahi nisichar kul ker ubaara ||
Jaasu doot bal barani na jaai |
Tehi aae pur kavan bhalaai ||

Dutinh san suni purajan baanee |
Mandodaree adhik akulaanee ||
Rahasi jori kar pati pag laagee |
Boli bachan neeti ras paagee ||
Kant karash hari san pariharahoo |
Mor kahaa ati hit hiy dharahoo ||
Samuzat jaasu doot kai karanee |
Stravahi garbh rajaneechar gharanee ||
Taasu naari nij sachiv bolaai |
Pathavahu kant jo chahahu bhalaai ||
Tav kul kamal bipin dukhadaai |
Sita Sit nisa sam aai ||
Sunahu naath sita binu deenhe |
Hit na tumhaar sambhu aj keenhe ||

|| Doha – 36 ||

Raam baan ahi gan saris nikar nisaachar bheka |

Jab lagi grasat na tab lagi jatanu karahu taji tek ||

||Chopai||

Shravan sunee sath taa kari baanee |
Bihasa jagat bidit abhimanee ||
Sabhay Subhaau naari kar saacha |

Mangal mahu bhay man ati kaacha ||
Jau aavai markat katakaai |
Jiahi bichaare nisichar khaai ||
Kampahi lokap jaakee traasa|
Taasu naari sabheet badi haasa||
As kahi bihasi taahi ur laai |
Chaleu sabha mamata adhikaai||
Mandodari hriday kar chinta | Bhayau kant par bidhi bipareeta
||
Baitheu sabha khabari asi paai |
Sindhu paar sena sab aai ||
Buzesi sachiv uchit mat kahahoo |
Te sab hanse masht kari rahahoo ||

Jitehu suraasur tab shram naahee |
Nar Baanar kehi lekhe maahee ||
|| Doha – 37 ||
Sachib baid gur teeni jau priy bolahi bhay aas |
Raaj dharm tan teeni kar hoi begihee naas ||

||Chopai||
Soi Raavan kahu bane sahaai |
Astuti karahi sunaai sunaai ||
Avasar jaani Bibheeshanu aava |
Bhrata charan seesu tehi naava ||
Puni siru naai baith nij aasan |
Bola bachan paai anusaasan ||
Jo krupaal poonchhihu mohi baata |
Mati anuroop kahau hit taata ||

Jo aapan chaahai kalyaana |
Sujasu sumati subh gati such nana ||

So parnaari lilaar gosaai |
Tajau chauthi ke chand ki naai ||
Chaudah bhuvan ek pati hoi |
Bhootadroh tishtai nahi soi ||
Gun saagar naagar nar jou |
Alap lobh bhal kahai na kou ||

|| Doha – 38 ||

Kaam krodh mad lobh sab nath narak ke panth |
Sab parihari Raghubeerahi bhajahu bhajau jehi sant ||

||Chopai||

Taat Raam nahi nar bhoopaala |
Bhuvaneshwar kaalahu kar kaala ||
Brahm anaamay aj bhagavanta |
Byapak ajit anaadi ananta ||
Go dwij dhenu dev hitakaaree |
Krupa sindhu manush tanudhaaree ||

Jan ranjan bhanjan khal braata |
Bed dharm rachchhak sunu bhrata ||
Tohi bayaru taji naaia maatha |
Pranataarati bhanjan Raghunaatha ||
Dehu naath prabhu kahu baidehee |
Bhajahu Raam binu hetu sanehee ||
Saran gae prabhu taahu na tyaaga |
Biswa droh krut agh jehi laaga ||
Jaasu naam tray taap nasavan |
Soi prabhu pragat samuzu jiy Raavan ||

|| Doha -39 ||

Baar baar pad laagau binay karau dasasees |
Parihari maan moh mad bhajahu kosalaadhees ||
Muni pulasti nij sisya san kahi pathai yah baat |
Turat so mai prabhu san kahee paai suavasaru taat||

||Chopai||

Malyavant ati sachiv sayaana |
Taasu bachan suni ati such maana ||
Taat anuj tav neeti Bibheeshan |
So ur dharahu jo kahat Bibheeshan ||
Ripu utakarash kahat sath dou |
Doori na karahu iha hai kou ||
Malyavant gruh gayau bahoree |
Kahai Bibheeshan puni kar joree ||
Sumati kumati sab ke ur rahahee |
Naath puran nigam as kahahee ||
Jaha sumati tah sampati nana |
Jaha kumati tah bipati nidaana ||
Tav ur kumati basi bipareeta |
Hit anahit maanahu ripu preeta ||
Kaalraati nisichar kul keree |
Tehi Sita par preeti ghaneree ||

|| Doha – 40 ||

Taat charan gahi maagau raakhahu mor dulaar|
Sita dehu Raam kahu ahit na hoi tumhaar ||

||Chopai||

Budh puraan shruti sammat baanee |
Kahi Bibheeshan neeti bakhanee ||
Sunat dasaanan utha risaai |
Khal tohi nikat mrutyu ab aai ||
Jiasi sada sath mor jiaava |
Ripu kar pachchha moodh tohi bhaava ||
Kahasi na khal as ko jag maahee |
Bhuj bal jaahi jita mai naahee ||
Mam pur basi tapasinh par preetee |
Sath milu jaai tinhahi kahu neetee ||
As kahi keenhesi charan prahaara |
Anuj gahe pad baarahi baara ||
Uma sant kai ihai badaai |

Mand karat jo karai bhalaai ||
Tumh pit saris bhalehi mohi maara |
Raamu bhaje hit naath tumhaara ||
Sachiv sang lai nabh path gayhaoo |
Sabahi sunaai kahat as bhayaoo ||

|| Doha – 41 ||

Raam satyasankalp prabhu sabha kaalbas tori |
Mai Raghubeer saran ab jaau dehu jani khori ||

||Chopai||

As kahi chala Bibheeshan jabahee |
Aayuheen bhae sab tabahee ||
Saadhu avagya turat bhavaanee |
Kar kalyaan akhil kai haanee ||
Raavan jabahi Bibheeshan tyaaga |

Bhayau bibhav binu tabahi abhaaga ||
Chaleu harashi Raghunaayak paahee |

Karat manorath bahu man maahee ||
Dekhihau jaai charan jalajaata |
Arun mrudul sevak sukhadaata ||
Je pad parasi taree rishinaaree |
Dandak Kaanan paavanakaaree ||
Je pad Janakasuta ur laae |
Kapat kurang sang dhar dhaae ||
Har ur sar saroj pad jei |
Ahobhagya mai dekhihau tei ||

|| Doha – 42 ||
Jinh paayanh ke paadukanhi bharatu rahe man laai|
Te pad aaju bilokihau inh nayananhi ab jaai ||

||Chopai||
Ehi bidhi karat saprem bichaara|
Aayau sapadi sindhu ehi paara ||
Kapinh Bibheeshan aavat dekha |

Jaana kou ripu doot bisesha ||
Taahi raakhi kapees pahi aae |
Samaachaar sab taahi sunaae ||
Kah Sugreev sunahu Raghuraai |
Aava Milan dasaanan bhaai ||
Kah prabhu sakha booziai kaaha |
Kahai kapees sunahu naranaaha ||
Jaani na jaai nisaachar maaya |
Kaamroop kehi kaaran aaya ||
Bhed Hamaar len sath aava |

Raakhia bandhi mohi as bhaava ||
Sakha neeti tumh neeki bichaaree |
Mam pan saranaagat bhayahaaree ||
Suni prabhu bachan harash Hanumaana |
Saranaagat bachchhal bhagawaana ||
|| Doha – 43 ||

Saranaagat kahu je tajahi nij anahit anumaanee |
Te nar paavar paapamay tinhahee bilokat haanee ||

||Chopai||
Koti bipra badh laagahi jaahoo |
Aae saran tajau nahi taahoo ||
Sanamukh hoi jeev mohi jabahee |
Janm koti agh naasahi tabahee ||
Paapavant kar sahaj subhaoo |
Bhajanu mor tehi bhaav na kaaoo ||
Jau pai dusht hriday soi hoi |
More sanamukh aav ki soi ||
Nirmal man jan so mohi paava |
Mohi kapat chhal chhidra na bhaava ||
Bhed len pathava dasaseesa |
Tabahu na kachu bhay haani kapeesa ||
Jag mahu sakha nisaachar jet e |
Lachhimanu hanai nimish mahu te te||

Jau sabheet aava saranaai |
Rakhihau taahi praan kee naai ||

|| Doha – 44 ||
Ubhay bhaanti tehi aanahu hasi kah krupaaniket |

Jay krupaal kahi kapi chale angad Hanoo samet ||

||Chopai||
Saadar tehi aage kari baanar |
Chale jaha Raghupati karunaakar ||
Doorihi te dekhe dwau bhraata |
Nayanaanand daan ke data ||
Bhuj pralamb kanjaarun lochan |
Syaamal gaat pranat bhay mochan ||
Singh kandh aayat ur soha |
Aanan amit madan man moha ||
Nayan neer pulakit ati gaata |
Man dhari dheer kahee mrudu baata ||

Naath dasaanan kar mai bhraata |
Nisichar bans janam suratraata ||
Sahaj paapapriy taamas deha |
Jatha ulukahi tam par neha ||
|| Doha – 45 ||
Shravan sujasu suni aayau prabhu bhanjan bhav bheer|
Traahi traahi aarati haran saran sukhad Rabhubeer ||

||Chopai||
As kahi karat dandavat dekha |
Turat uthe prabhu harash bisesha ||
Deen bachan suni prabhu man bhaava |
Bhuj bisaal gahi hriday lagaava ||
Anuj sahit mili dhig baithaaree|
Bole bachan bhagat bhayaharree ||

Kahu Lankes sahit parivaara |
Kusal kuthaahar baas tumhaara ||

Khal mandalee basahu dinu raatee |
Sakha dharam nibahai kehi bhaantee ||
Mai jaanau tumhaari sab reetee |
Ati nay nipun na bhaav aneetee ||
Baru bhal baas narak kar taata |
Dusht sang jani dei bidhaata ||
Ab pad dekhi kusal Raghuraaya |
Jau tumh keenhi jaani jan daaya ||
|| Doha – 46 ||
Tab lagi kusal na jeev kahu sapane hu man bishraam|
Jab lagi bhajat na Raam kahu sok dhaam taji kaam ||

||Chopai||
Tab lagi hriday basat khal nana |
Lobh moh machchhar mad maana ||
Jab lagi ur na basat Raghunaatha|
Dhare chaap saayak kati bhaatha ||

Mamata tarun tamee adhiaaree |
Raag dvesh ulook sukhakaaree ||
Tab lagi basati jeev man maahee |
Jab lagi prabhu prataap rabi naahee ||
Ab mai kusal mite bhay bhaare |
Dekhi Raam pad kamal tumhaare ||
Tumh krupaal jaa par anukoola |
Taahi na byaap tribidh bhav soola ||
Mai nisichar ati adham subhaaoo |

Subh aacharanu keenh nahi kaaoo ||
Jaasu roop muni dhyaan na aava |
Tehi prabhu harashi hriday mohi lava||

|| Doha – 47 ||

Ahobhagya mama amita ati rama krpa sukha punja|
Dekhe'um nayana biranci siva sebya jugala pada kanja||

||Chopai||

Sunahu sakha nija kaha'um subha'u. Jana bhusundi sambhu girija'u||
Jaum nara ho'i caracara drohi. Avai sabhaya sarana taki mohi||
Taji mada moha kapata chala nana.
Kara'um sadya tehi sadhu samana||
Janani janaka bandhu suta dara.
Tanu dhanu bhavana suhrda parivara||
Saba kai mamata taga batori. Mama pada manahi bamdha bari dori||
Samadarasi iccha kachu nahim.
Harasa soka bhaya nahim mana mahim||
Asa sajjana mama ura basa kaisem.
Lobhi hrdayam basa'i dhanu jaisem||
Tumha sarikhe santa priya morem.
Dhara'um deha nahim ana nihorem||

|| Doha – 48 ||

Sagun upaasak parahit nirat neeti dradh nem|

Te nar praan samaan mam jinh ke dvij pad prem||

||Chopai||

Sunu Lankesh sakal gun tore |
Taate tumh atisay priy more ||
Raam bachan suni baanar jootha |
Sakal kahahi jay krupa barootha ||
Sunat Bibheeshanu prabhu kai baanee |
Nahi aghaat shravanaamrut jaanee ||
Pad Ambuj gahi baarahi baara |
Hriday samaat na premu apaara ||
Sunahu dev sacharaachar swamee |
Pranatapaal ur antarajaamee ||
Ur kachhu pratham baasana rahee |
Prabhu pad preeti sarit so bahee ||
Ab krupaal nij bhagat paavanee |
Dehu sada siv man bhaavanee ||
Evamastu kahi prabhu ranadheera |

Maaga turat sindhu kar neera ||
Jadapi sakha tav ichchha naahee |
Mor darasu amogh jag maahee ||
As kahi Raam tilak tehi saara |
Suman brushti nabh bhai apaara ||

|| Doha – 49 ||

Raavan krodh anal nij svaas sameer prachand |
Jarat Bibheeshan raakheu
deenheu raaju akhand ||
Jo sampati siv ravanahi deenhi die das math |
Soi sampada Bibheeshanhi sakuchi deenhi Raghunaath ||

||Chopai||

As prabhu chhadi bhajahi je aana |
Te nar pasu binu poonch bishaata ||
Nij jan jaani taahi apanaava |
Prabhu subhaav kapi kul man bhaava ||

Puni sarbagya sarb ur baasee |
Sarbaroop sab rahit udaasee ||
Bole bachan neeti pratipaalak |
Kaaran manuj danuj kul ghaalk ||
Sunu kapees Lankaapati bera |
Kehi bidhi taria jaladhi gambheera ||
Sankul maker urag zash jaatee |
Ati agaadh duster sab bhaantee ||
Kah Lankesh sunahu Raghunaayak |
Koti sindhu soshak tav saayak ||
Jadyapi tadapi neeti asi gaai |
Binay karia saagar san jaai ||

|| Doha – 50 ||

Prabhu tumhaar kulagur jaladhi kahihi upaay bichaari|
Binu prayaas saagar tarihi sakal bhaalu kapi dhaari ||

||Chopai||

Sakha kahee tumh neeki upaai |
Karia daiv jau hoi sahaai ||
Mantra na yah lachhiman man bhaava |
Raam bachan suni ati dookh paava ||
Naath daiv kar kavan bharosa |
Soshia sindhu karia man rosa ||
Kaadar man kahu ek adhara |

Daiv daiv aalasee pukaara | |
Sunat bihasi bole raghubeera |
Aisehi karab dharahu man dheera | |
As kahi prabhu anujahi samuzaai |
Sindhu sameep gae Raghuraai | |
Pratham pranaam keenh siru naai |
Baithe puni tat darbh dasaai | |
Jabahi bibheeshan prabhu pahi aae |
Paachhe raavan doot pathaae | |

|| Doha – 51 ||
Sakal charit tinh dekhe dhare kapat kapi deh |
Prabhu gun hriday saraahahi sarnaagat par neh| |

||Chopai||
Pragat bakhaanahi Raam subhaaoo|
Ati saprem gaa bisari duraaoo | |
Ripu ke doot kapinh tab jaane |
Sakal baandhi kapees pahi aane | |
Kah Sugreev sunahu sab baanar |
Ang bhang kari pathavahu nisichar| |
Suni Sugreev bachan kapi dhaae |
Deen pukaarat tadapi na tyaage | |
Jo hamaar har naasa kaana |
Tehi kosalaadhees kai aana | |
Suni lachhiman sab nikat bolaae |
Daya laagi hasi turat chhodaae | |
Raavan kar deejahu yah paatee |

Lachhiman bachan baachu kulaghaatee| |

|| Doha – 52 ||

kahehu mukhaagar moodh san mam sandesu udaar |
Sita dei milahu na ta aava kaalu tumhaar ||

||Chopai||

Turat naai lachhiman pad maatha |
Chale doot baranat gun gaatha ||
Kahat Raam jasu Lanka aae |
Raavan charan sees tinh naae ||
Bihasi dasaanan poonchhee baata |
Kahasi na suk aapani kusalaata ||
Puni kahu khabari Bibheeshan keree|
Jaahi mryutu aai ati neree ||
Karat raaj Lanka sath tyaagee |
Hoihi jav kar keet abhaagee ||
Puni kahu bhaalu kees katakaai |

Kathin kaal prerit chali aai ||
Jinh ke jeevan kar rakhavaara |
Bhayau mrudul chit sindhu bichaara ||
Kahu tapasinh kai baat bahoree |
Jinh ke hriday traas ati moree ||

|| Doha – 53 ||

Kee bhai bhet ki firi gae shravan sujasu suni mor |
Kahasi na ripu dal tej bal bahut chakit chit tor ||

||Chopai||

Naath krupa kari poonchhehu jaise |
Maanahu kahaa krodh taji taise ||
Mila jaai jab anuj tumhaara |

Jaatahi raam tilak tehi saara ||
Raavan doot hamahi suni kaana |
Kapinh baandhi deenhe dukh nana ||
Shravan naasika kaatai laage |

Raam sapath deenhe ham tyaage ||
Poonchhehu naath Raam katakaai |
Badan koti sat barani na jaai ||
Naana baran bhaalu kapi dhaaree |
Bikataanan bisaal bhayakaaree ||
Jehi pur daheu hateu sut tora |
Sakal kapinh mah tehi balu thora||
Amit naam bhat kathin karaala |
Amit naag bal bipul bisaala ||

|| Doha – 54 ||

Dwibid mayank neel nal angad gad bikataasi |
Dadhi mukh kehari nisath sat jaamavant balaraasi ||

||Chopai||

E kapi sab Sugreev samaana |
Inh sam kotinh ganai ko nana ||
Raam krupa atulit bal tinhahee |

Trun samaan trailokahi ganahee ||
As mai suna shravan dasakandhar |
Padum atharah juthap Bandar ||
Naath katak mah so kapi naahee |
Jo na tumhahi jetai ran maahee ||
Param krodh meejahi sab haatha |
Aayasu pain a dehi raghunaatha ||
Soshahi sindhu sahit zash byaala |

Poorahi na ta bhari kudhar bisaala ||
Mardi gard milavahi dasaseesa |
Aisei bachan kahahi sab keesa ||
Garjahi tarjahi sahaj asanka |
Maanahu grasan chahat hahi Lanka ||
|| Doha – 55 ||
Sahaj soor kapi bhaalu sab puni sir par prabhu Raam |
Raavan kaal koti kahu jeeti sakahi sangraam ||

||Chopai||
Raam tej bal budhi bipulaai |
Sesh sahas sat sakahi na gaai ||
Sak sar ek soshi sat saagar |
Tav bhraatahi poonchheu nay naagar ||
Taasu bachan sni saagar paahee |
Maagat panth krupa man maahee ||
Sunat bachan bihasa dasaseesa |
Jau asi mati sahaay krut keesa ||
Sahaj bheeru kar bachan dhradhaai|
Saagar san thaanee machalaai ||
Moodh mrusha kaa karasi badai |
Ripu bal buddhi thaah mai paai ||
Sachiv sabheet Bibheeshan jaake |
Bijay bibhooti kahaa jag take ||
Suni khal bachan doot ris baadhee |
Samay bichaari patrika kaadhee ||

Raamaanuj deenhee yah paatee |
Nath bachaai judaavahu chhatee ||
Bihasi baam kar leenhee Raavan |

Sachiv boli sath laag bachaavan ||
|| Doha – 56 ||
Baatanh manahi rizaai sath jani ghaalasi kul khees |
Raam birodh na ubarasi saran bishnu aj is ||
Kee taji maan anuj iv prabhu pad pankaj bhrung |
Hohi ki Raam saraanal khal kul sahit patang ||

||Chopai||
Sunat sabhay man much musukaai |
Kahat dasaanan sabahi sunaai ||
Bhoomi para kar gahat akaasa|
Laghu taapas kr bag bilaasa ||
Kah suk naath satya sb baanee |
Samuzahu chhadi prakruti abhimaanee ||

Sunau bachan mam parihari krodha |
Naath Raam san tajahu birodha ||
Ati komal Raghubeer subhaaoo |
Jadhyapi akhil lok kar raaoo ||
Milat krupa tumh par prabhu karihee |
Ur aparaadh na ekau dharihee ||
Janaksuta Raghenaathhi deeje |
Etana kaha mor prabhu keeje ||
Jab tehi kahaa den baidehee |
Charan prahaar keenh sath tejee ||
Naai charan siru chala so tahaa|
Krujpasindhu Raghunaayak jahaa ||
Kari pranaam nij katha sunaai |
Raam krupa aapani gati paai ||
Rishi agasti kee saap bhavaanee |

Raachhas bhayau raha muni gyaanee ||
Bandi Raam pad baarahi baara |

Muni nij aashram kahu pagu dhaara ||
|| Doha – 57 ||
Binay na maanat jaladhi jad gae teeni din beeti |
Bole Raam sakop tab bhay binu hoi na preeti ||

||Chopai||
Lachhiman baan saraasan aanu |
Soshau baaridhi bisikh krusaanoo ||
Sath san binay kutil san preetee |
Sahaj krupan san sundar neetee ||
Mamata rat san gyaan kahaanee |
Ati lobhee san birati bakhaanee ||
Krodhihi sam kaamihi harikatha |
Oosar beej bae fal jatha ||
As kahi Raghupati chhap chadhaava |
Yah mat lachhiman ke man bhaava ||
Sandhaaneu prabhu bisikh karaala |

Uthi udadhi ur antar jwaala ||
Makar urag zash gan akulaane |
Jarat jantu jalanidhi jab jaane ||
Kanak thaar bhari mani gan nana |
Bipra roop aayau taji maana ||
|| Doha – 58 ||
Kaatehin Pai Kadaree Phari Koti Jatan Kou Seench|
Binay Na Maan Khages Sunu Daatehin Pai Nav Neech||

||Chopai||

Sabhay Sindhu Gahi Pad Prabhu Kere.
Chhamahu Naath Sab Avagun Mere||
Gagan Sameer Anal Jal Dharanee. Inh Kai Naath Sahaj Jad Karanee||
Tav Prerit Maayaan Upajae.
Srshti Hetu Sab Granthani Gae||
Prabhu Aayasu Jehi Kahan Jas Ahee.
So Tehi Bhaanti Rahen Sukh Lahee||

Prabhu Bhal Keenh Mohi Sikh Deenheen.
Marajaada Puni Tumharee Keenheen||
Dhol Gavaanr Soodr Pasu Naaree.
Sakal Taadana Ke Adhikaaree||
Prabhu Prataap Main Jaab Sukhaee.
Utarihi Kataku Na Mori Badaee||
Prabhu Agya Apel Shruti Gaee.
Karaun So Begi Jo Tumhahi Sohaee||

|| Doha – 59 ||

Sunat Bineet Bachan Ati Kah Krpaal Musukai|
Jehi Bidhi Utarai Kapi Kataku Taat So Kahahu Upai||

||Chopai||

Naath Neel Nal Kapi Dvau Bhae.
Larikaeen Rishi Aasish Paee||
Tinh Ken Paras Kien Giri Bhaare.
Tarihahin Jaladhi Prataap Tumhaare||

Main Puni Ur Dhari Prabhu Prabhutaee. Karihun Bal Anumaan Sahaee||
Ehi Bidhi Naath Payodhi Bandhai.

Jehin Yah Sujasu Lok Tihun Gai||
Ehi Sar Mam Uttar Tat Baasee.
Hatahu Naath Khal Nar Agh Raasee||
Suni Krpaal Saagar Man Peera.
Turatahin Haree Raam Ranadheera||
Dekhi Raam Bal Paurush Bhaaree.
Harashi Payonidhi Bhayu Sukhaaree||
Sakal Charit Kahi Prabhuhi Sunaava.
Charan Bandi Paathodhi Sidhaava||

|| Chhand ||
Nij Bhavan Gavaneu Sindhu Shreeraghupatihi Yah Mat Bhaayoo|
Yah Charit Kali Mal Har Jathaamati Daas Tulasee Gaayoo||
Sukh Bhavan Sansay Saman
Davan Bishaad Raghupati Gun Gana|

Taji Sakal Aas Bharos Gaavahi Sunahi Santat Sath Mana||
|| Doha – 60 ||
Sakal sumangal daayak Raghunaayak gun gaan |
Saadar sunahi te tarahi bhav sindhu bina jalajaan ||

Printed in Great Britain
by Amazon

38387187R00030